LABRADOR CINEMA

MARK DAVID TURNER   MORGEN MILLS

ISBN 978-1-7782193-0-6
Second printing

Design and layout: Graham Blair
Cover design: Perfect Day
Map design: Morgen Mills
Printed in Canada by Type A Print

Published by Brack and Brine with support from the Newfoundland and Labrador Film Development Corporation and the Labrador Campus of Memorial University

Inquiries regarding *Labrador Cinema* may be directed to Brack and Brine:
PO Box 1713 Stn B, Happy Valley-Goose Bay, NL A0P 1E0 Canada

www.brackandbrine.com

Newfoundland & Labrador Film Development Corporation

Memorial University Labrador Campus

for my brother, David Turner, and my sister, Suzanne Turner

—MDT

for Beatrix

—MM

CONTENTS

ACKNOWLEDGEMENTS

This book explores representations of Labrador, including the homelands and territories of Innu, Inuit, and their forebears. We respectfully acknowledge the Indigenous cultures, languages, histories, and futures with which we have engaged. Most of the work leading to this book's publication has been carried out in Labrador and with Labrador people, to whom we owe a great debt of gratitude.

Labrador Cinema arises from the 2011-2017 Labrador/ians on Film screening series hosted in Happy Valley-Goose Bay by Memorial University's Labrador Institute (now the Labrador Campus), with programming principally developed by Mark and screenings coordinated by Morgen. Jennifer Butler-Wight encouraged us to develop the series and hosted early events, and Jon Beale coordinated the series from 2011-2012. Financial support for Labrador/ians on Film was generously provided by the Labrador Institute under directors Keith Chaulk and Ashlee Cunsolo. Martha MacDonald provided invaluable guidance in curating the series and developing program notes, and Beatrice Dickers ensured the administrative operation of the series.

The idea to develop this book first emerged at the 2017 Labrador Research Forum, where we officially concluded Labrador/ians on Film. The support of the Labrador Institute was instrumental for the early development of the manuscript. We are also grateful to Chris Bonnell, Dorian Rowe, and Laura Churchill of the Newfoundland and Labrador Film Development Corporation for their encouragement to develop the book, and for financial support.

Much like filmmaking, when done properly the creation of a book is a collaborative undertaking requiring contributions and supports from many quarters. We are especially indebted to all those who have provided us with image permissions, information, advice, ideas, and feedback over the past five years while we have put this book together:

Joan Andersen
Andersen family
Carolyn Atkinson
Leander Baikie
Kat Baulu
Roberta Benefiel
Elizabeth Bowley
Anne Budgell
Brenda Carroll
Aimee Chaulk
Hannie Fitzgerald
Norma Flynn
Tom Gordon
James Gorton
Navarana Igloliorte
Susan Kaplan
Genevieve LeMoine
Gillian Levene
Stephen Loring
Eva Luther
Marguerite MacKenzie
Nigel Markham
Ragnhild Milewski
Neil McCormick
Sandy Newton
OKâlaKatiget Society
Tim McNeill
Christine Poker
Fiona Polack
Donna Roberts
Sandra Ronayne
Sarah Sandring
Denise Stevens
Vollprecht Family
Linda White
Fran Williams
Joan Wulff

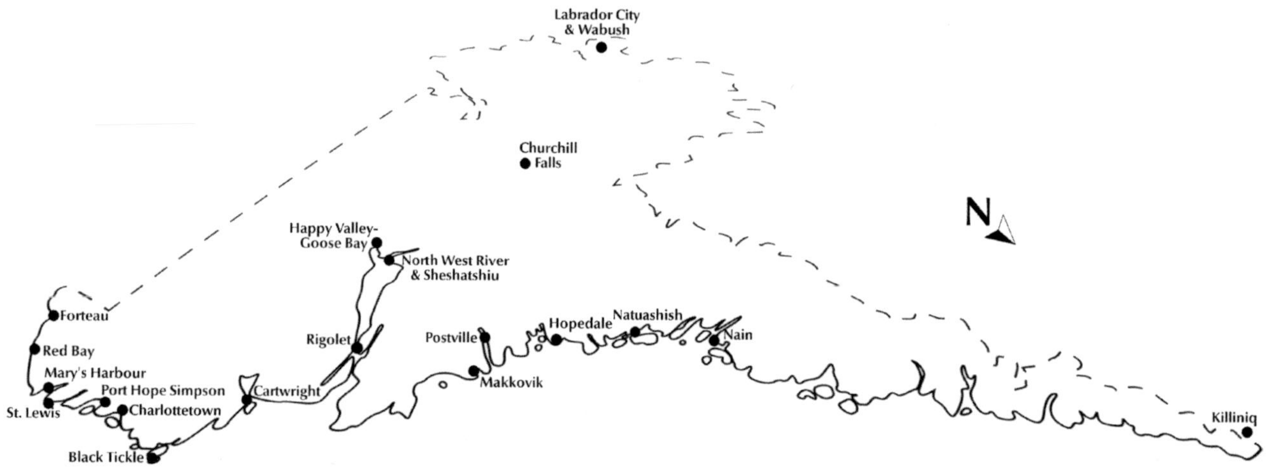

An illustration of Labrador's geography, drawing on spatial perspectives suggested by the cinema.

INTRODUCTION

This is a book about Labrador's relationship with moving imagery. We have written it for the people of Labrador first of all, and also for other readers interested in cinema and the North. Our purpose is to locate this place and its people as active agents in a long history of moving image-making. "Every image embodies a way of seeing," the English art critic John Berger tells us.[1] That way of seeing has three points: the viewer, the photographer, and the subject. Our focus here is principally on Labrador's role as subject.

There are many ideas of Labrador. Elizabeth Goudie wrote in *Woman of Labrador*, for example, that "the name Labrador holds something hard to explain but I would like to explain it in my own way, and that is peace—a deep peace within."[2] Labrador is also a space on the north-eastern edge of North America, politically defined by borders with the province of Quebec to the south and west, the territory of Nunavut to the north, and the Labrador Sea to the east. It is the mainland portion of today's province of Newfoundland and Labrador, in Canada. Its present borders bisect the Innu homeland of Ntesinan and contain the Inuit homelands of Nunatsiavut and NunatuKavut. Within those borders are also diverse settler communities. In many parts of coastal Labrador, the term Settler, or Kablunângajuit, historically referred to people of mixed Inuit and European ancestry. Alongside these Settlers are other people originating from many countries.

Cinema is equally difficult to define. For this book, we have taken a broad view, following Canadian film critic Jerry White's concept of "any form of moving-image arts."[3] The type of media—television, film, video tape, computer screen—does not really matter. Locally produced media constitute a cinema because they provide opportunities for shared cultural experiences. In this book, we expand our understanding to include all moving imagery that concerns Labrador and its people, in part because until recently there have been few opportunities for communities to screen media that concern them, and fewer opportunities still to share such media with other communities in the region.

Such an understanding cannot be used widely. Three things distinguish Labrador. First is its size: 294,330 km^2. It is, as local broadcaster Winston White called it, "The Big Land." Second is its diversity. Its 27,000 people make up three different Indigenous cultures and diverse settler cultures. Many languages are spoken, and Innu-aimun, Inuttitut/Inuttut, and English are all widely used. Third, Labrador is distantly removed from any centre of state power. These things have rendered Labrador exotic in the outside imagination, and so there has long been a premium on its representation. This also means that the relationship between subject and filmmaker is different in Labrador, because Labradorians have understood this premium from the beginning. Far from being passive subjects, they exert uncommon agency in their own representation.

There is a stylistic consequence to this exoticism. Labrador's cinema overwhelmingly belongs to the documentary tradition. Of the nearly two hundred productions we record in our filmography—this tally does not include individual television episodes—there are only a handful that do not chronicle some expedition, event, individual, or point of interest. At the time of this writing, there remains, to our knowledge, no emerging tradition of narrative filmmaking.

The pre-eminence of documentary filmmaking is also part of a clear tendency in Labrador to favour all forms of documentary media that concern this place and the people. In our current historical moment, we could tidily think of this larger tendency as a product of colonialism. Labradorians have historically been under-represented within British, Newfoundland, and Canadian governance, and documentary forms provide a direct and cost-effective mechanism to represent oneself. But we think this is far too simplistic and allows little for Labradorians' own creative agency. From the beginnings of Labrador cinema in 1901 with the filmed ethnographic performances of Esther Eneutseak, Simon Aputik, Zacharias Zad, and other Labrador Inuit, there is a clear sophistication in how and what Labradorians communicate in documentary film. This sophistication comes from literacy in documentary convention and precise knowledge of how Labrador has been represented and interpreted in documentary film and elsewhere. Labrador's documentary tradition is also influenced by a regional preference arising from the skill, expertise, and cultural context of its local creators and subjects.

Filmmaking is only part of what we consider to be Labrador cinema. Film-watching plays an important role as well. While population centres like Happy Valley-Goose Bay, Labrador City, and Churchill Falls each had purpose built theatres from their beginnings, access to moving images has been sporadic in every other community. Along Labrador's coast, the first moving picture show likely took place in Nain in 1927 when Donald Baxter MacMillan screened footage that he had taken in northern Labrador and northern Greenland.[4] Anecdotally, we also know that Canadian and US naval personnel invited residents from coastal communities aboard their vessels to watch films during World War II. After the war, independent projectionists in communities such as Nain and Makkovik provided screenings in community halls. Hopedale residents were able to watch films in a purpose-built theatre at the General Surveillance Radar Station operated by the United States Air Force from 1953 to 1968. Local preference was for Westerns. Beginning in the late 1960s, canned television and video tapes were circulated throughout the entire region by organizations such as the Memorial University's Extension Service and the Canadian Broadcasting Corporation's Northern Television Service, until they were superseded by cable television in the 1990s.

Because of its complexity, we feel the best way to begin to understand Labrador cinema is through its visible record and not a lengthy, textual interpretation of that record. The thirteen chapters that make up this book are arranged according to decade. Each includes imagery from films, filmmaking, or film-watching in Labrador. We have selected images that we believe show how Labrador cinema has developed. We recognize that for some Labrador readers, this will mean that we have excluded some films that are significant in other ways. However, at the end of this book we have included a detailed, chronological filmography that will allow you to place all the films we discuss in their production context.

Many of the films we consider here are available at Memorial University's Labrador Campus in Happy Valley-Goose Bay. We encourage you to visit and watch them.

1900s

Although motion picture technology had its advent in the 1890s, there is no evidence to suggest that moving images were made in Labrador prior to the 1910s. However, Labrador Inuit working in the United States blazed trails on both sides of early cameras. Four of these Inuit ethnographic performers are well documented: Esther Eneutseak and Zacharias Zad of Zoar, Simon Aputik of Okak, and Eneutseak's daughter Columbia Eneutseak, widely known as Nancy Columbia, "the World's Fair Baby." They were accompanied on screen by many other Labrador Inuit in films made by the Edison, S. Lubin, and American Mutoscope and Biograph companies during the 1901 Pan-American Exposition in Buffalo, New York. Many of these Inuit returned to Labrador towards the end of the decade, but Eneutseak and Columbia stayed and cultivated successful film careers into the 1910s.

In nineteenth-century ethnographic exhibitions, people from Indigenous and foreign cultures performed choreographed versions of ordinary daily activities or cultural practices for audiences across Europe and North America. This film captures a demonstration of whip work. On the left side of the screen a performer, possibly Zacharias Zad, looks directly at the camera. Midway through the 25-second film, he walks across the screen, smoking, with a wry expression suggesting that he understands he is upstaging the action.

Esquimaux Game of Snap-the-Whip, frame enlargement
1901, dir. Edwin S. Porter, Edison Company
LIBRARY OF CONGRESS CONTROL NUMBER 00694349

The leap-froggers are framed to the left by an Inuk who keeps rhythm with a small whip and to the right by a white man (perhaps Ralph Taber, the group's promoter) who oversees the performance. Behind, we see the full incongruity of the so-called "Esquimaux Village." Power lines and smokestacks hover overhead. The set is a surreal composition of angles, shadows, and textures.

Esquimaux Leap-Frog, frame enlargement
1901, dir. Edwin S. Porter, Edison Company
LIBRARY OF CONGRESS CONTROL NUMBER 00694350

The frame provides us with a closer look at the construction of the "Esquimaux Village" in Buffalo. The texture of the ground is meant to approximate snow, but in the wake of the Komatik, you can see a trail of dust. This Exposition ran through the summer, from May to November, and conditions in the parkas must have been sweltering.

The Esquimaux Village, frame enlargement
1901, dir. Edwin S. Porter, Edison Company
LIBRARY OF CONGRESS CONTROL NUMBER 000694348

Labrador Inuit were remarkably well-documented at the 1901 Buffalo Pan-American Exposition. The pioneering American photographer and photojournalist Frances Benjamin Johnston took this picture at the Esquimaux Village. In a candid moment, here a woman and child sit on a traditionally constructed Komatik, while a man works with a bone-handled saw. The clear focus on people distracts from the looming pavilion at the top of the frame.

Esquimaux Village, photograph
1901, Frances Benjamin Johnston
LIBRARY OF CONGRESS CONTROL NUMBER 2005691849

1910s

Esther Eneutseak and Nancy Columbia's run in the American film industry culminated with two feature films shot in Escabana, Michigan, in 1910. Released in 1911, *The Way of the Eskimo* and *Lost in the Arctic* are now considered lost, but they are exceptional within the story of Labrador's cinema, as many Labrador Inuit held the principal roles in both films. Nancy Columbia also wrote the scenario for *The Way of the Eskimo*, making her the first screenwriter of Labrador descent.

It is likely that the first film shot in Labrador was taken by American businessman, hunter, and documentarian Paul J. Rainey during an expedition led by Captain Bob Bartlett to the northeastern Arctic in 1911.[5] The only film that remains from that expedition comes from Greenland.

Two years later, an expedition from the Carnegie Institute in Pittsburgh set out on a three-month journey along Labrador's north coast and into Ungava Bay. "The trip," the *Pittsburgh Post-Gazette* reported at the time, "was made for the purpose of showing, through moving picture, the life of the Labrador Eskimo and Indian and for gathering lecture data of life and legends in the semi-barbaric wilderness."[6] Cameraman Alfred Ward Birdsall presented his footage as part of an illustrated lecture called *Through Eskimo Land,* which he gave throughout the American northeast in 1914.

The earliest surviving moving images of Labrador itself were taken by Harold Wyckoff and Bill Derr in 1919, when they travelled aboard the Hudson's Bay Company ship *RMS Nacopie*, shooting for a film celebrating the 250th anniversary of the HBC, *Romance of the Far Fur Country*.

Released July 17, 1911

THE WAY OF THE ESKIMO

PRODUCED BY
WILLIAM V. MONG

CAST

Ananak, *an Eskimo Maiden*	Cloumbia
Tikatak, *her Mother*	Enutisak
OPETEK, *her Father and chief of the tribe*	Chief Opetek
Zak, *her Lover*	Zachariah
Joe Turner, *Trappers*	William V. Mong
Tom Hurd, *Trappers*	J. C. Smith

THE WAY OF THE ESKIMO opens with an altogether unique scene in Picturedom... A tribe of Labrador Eskimos are seen in their peculiar ceremony of bidding the sun good-bye. It is called "The Feast of the Adieu to the Sun".

Zak, a young Eskimo belonging to a tribe far removed from the village of old Chief Opetek and his family where the ceremony takes place, is one of the participants, he is visiting his sweetheart, the daughter of the chief. When the sun has disappeared Zak says "Good-bye" and starts, with his dog team, on his homeward journey over the ice. He comes upon a half frozen hunter—a white man—back to the village and into the hut of the chief the stranger is taken, cared for and nursed back to life. Zak again prepares to depart for home and, according to the Eskimo fashion of greeting and leave taking among near and dear ones, smells the sleeves of and rubs noses with his sweetheart. After he has gone, and during the absence of the girl's parents from the hut, the white man ridicules the Eskimo method of bestowing caresses and shows her the white man's way of making love. The old chief and his wife enter the hut in time to see the daughter elope with the stranger.

Winter has passed. Zak launches his kiack or canoe and starts upon his journey by water to the village of his sweetheart. His meeting with his sweetheart whom the white man long since deserted, their entrance into the summer village of old chief Opetek,—the strange marriage ceremony of the Eskimos—portrayed by the natives themselves in their far off land make up an historical romance of peculiar value to the film world.

LENGTH, ABOUT 995 FEET CODE WORD, "AJADAS"

PRODUCED AND CONTROLLED EXCLUSIVELY BY
The SELIG POLYSCOPE CO., Inc.
20 E. Randolph St. CHICAGO, U. S. A.
Licensees of the Motion Picture Patents Co.

Have you

The Way of the Eskimo was a silent film, advertised as "about 995 feet" long, or roughly 10 minutes. Nancy Columbia, at the centre of this promotional image, performed the role of "Ananak, an Eskimo maiden." Anânak means "mother" in Inuttitut/Inuttut, somewhat ironically given that beside Columbia stands her own mother, Esther Eneutseak, who played Ananak's mother Tikatak in the film. The group is posing in front of a painted backdrop with vistas of ice and mountains reminiscent of the "Esquimaux Village" from the Buffalo Pan-American Exposition.

The Way of the Eskimo, release flyer and promotional image
1911, Selig Polyscope Company
MARGARET HERRICK LIBRARY, ACADEMY OF MOTION PICTURE ARTS AND SCIENCES

THE **GRAND** OPERA HOUSE

THURSDAY FRIDAY SATURDAY

JAN. 15-16-17

Extraordinary Picture Attraction

THE CELEBRATED LECTURER **ALFRED WARD BIRDSALL** WITH 15,000 FEET OF MOTION PICTURES ON A TRAVEL

"Through Eskimo Land"

Thrilling Scenes of the Great Nothern Country

SEE THE CAPTURE OF A MAMMOTH WHALE
THE MIGHTY HUNTERS
THE ANIMALS OF THE POLAR REGIONS

A Prominent Official of the P. & I. E. R. R. saw the Pictures at the Nixon Theatre, Pittsburgh, and pronounced it the Best Exhibit He Had Ever Seen.

PRICES:--Matinee 25c. Night 25c & 50c. Matinees Daily. All Seats at Night Reserved

This advertisement ran in *The Morning Herald* from Uniontown, Pennsylvania, on January 12th, 1914. The image of Hopedale on the left side is all that remains of Alfred Ward Birdsall's footage of Labrador. Though blurry, you can make out the markings of the Moravian church with its bell tower in the upper right hand side of the frame. Footage of Hopedale in the 1952 documentary *Big Island* shows the residential architecture unchanged.

Through Eskimo Land, advertisement
THE MORNING HERALD, UNIONTOWN, PENNSYLVANIA, JANUARY 12, 1914, PAGE 2

ATLANTIC
LAKE HARBOUR
PORT BURWELL
WOLSTENHOLME
CAPE CHIDLEY
HUDSON
BAY
CANADA
LABRADOR
CHARLTON ISLAND
MOOSE FACTORY
NEW POST
WINNIPEG
MONTREAL
UNITED
STATES

Romance of the Far Fur Country, also recut as *The Heritage of Adventure*, visualizes the voyage of the *S.S. Nascopie* from many perspectives, bringing the viewer progressively closer to the north. The image of Killiniq here, taken by Harold Wyckoff and Bill Derr, is a still from the only known footage of the settlement.

The Heritage of Adventure, frame enlargement
1919, Hudson's Bay Company
HUDSON'S BAY COMPANY ARCHIVES, ARCHIVES OF MANITOBA, HB2011/1

1920s

The explorer-filmmakers of the 1920s perfected an approach to Labrador that had been developed in the 1910s. Varick Frissell's *Lure of the Labrador* (1926) contained the first film footage of the Grand Falls. Frissell was widely celebrated for this film and has the distinction of being the only filmmaker to have a street named after him in either Labrador or Newfoundland: Frissell Street in Churchill Falls.

Two years after the release of *Lure of the Labrador*, another American, Howard Taylor, led another expedition to the Grand Falls by a route along Rivière Saint-Jean, Quebec.[7] A copy of that expedition footage survives at the Smithsonian Institution in Washington, DC, as *Unknown Falls: John Kernan's Exploration in Central Labrador*, named for the expedition's cameraman.

Further north, in 1927, a scientific expedition led by the American Donald Baxter MacMillan to Anaktalak Bay was also taking documentary footage. His footage of the first Model-T snowmobile in Labrador, which dates to this time, is widely recognized by Labradorians today. Also on the north coast, the Hettasch family of Moravian missionaries began shooting film and would continue into the 1960s.

Varick Frissell's three surviving films are defined by imagery both perilous and sublime. While *Lure of the Labrador* is celebrated for presenting the first images of Churchill Falls, Frissell's visual accomplishment in the film comes during the return journey to North West River. Here, he films as his canoe runs a stretch of rapids.

The Lure of the Labrador, frame enlargement
1926, dir. Varick Frissell

Varick Frissell at work on location, likely in southern Labrador, or possibly in northern Newfoundland, circa 1926-1930. This image was not taken during the filming of *Lure of the Labrador*, meaning that what we see here is Frissell in production for either *The Great Arctic Seal Hunt* or the film that would claim his life, *White Thunder*.

photograph

ARCHIVES & SPECIAL COLLECTIONS, MEMORIAL UNIVERSITY

John Kernan was able to capture one angle of the Grand Falls that Frissell did not. Anyone familiar with the falls will recognize this perspective, but this is its first appearance in a moving image.

Unknown Falls: John Kernan's Exploration in Central Labrador, frame enlargement
1928
HUMAN STUDIES FILM ARCHIVES, SMITHSONIAN INSTITUTION

1930s

By the 1930s, all regions of Labrador had been represented on film. The proliferation of cameras that were smaller and easier to operate meant an increase in the diversity of moving imagery from the region. In the west, an expedition led by James S. Wishart produced the first aerial footage of Labrador, which now exists as part of *Dr. Wishart's Labrador Journey*. In the south, Louis Twyeffort shot film at the nursing station in Spotted Island: footage that was likely incorporated into illustrated lectures given by the Grenfell Mission to raise funds for their work in Labrador and northern Newfoundland. The Grenfell Mission would become one of the most prolific film producers in Labrador. And in the north, Captain Bob Bartlett partnered with American cameraman Maurice Kellerman, who also filmed Varick Frissell's *The Viking*, to produce a number of films for British Pathé featuring Labrador Inuit.

Outside the Spotted Island nursing station, 1932. To the right of the frame, Louis Twyeffort kneels and films beside his wife, Elizabeth. To his left are Mr. Petten the schoolteacher and Jack Holwell with a balloon in hand. This is a rare picture of the camera in operation during the early years of filmmaking in Labrador.

photograph

1932

DR. LOUIS H. TWYEFFORT AND ELIZABETH B. TWYEFFORT COLLECTION

COURTESY OF SUSAN T. SPOOR

One of the most prolific makers of moving imagery in Labrador was Catholic priest Edward O'Brien. In 1914 the Diocese assigned him to the community of Northern Bay in Newfoundland, whose parish included Labrador. O'Brien first travelled to North West River and Davis Inlet in 1921 for pastoral work, and he continued to visit both communities until Labrador was set up as its own parish in 1946. Between 1928 and 1940, he shots dozens of hours of footage in and around these communities. Unfortunately, today little of his material is well-described or easily accessible. This image, which features O'Brien amongst his Innu parishioners, comes from a short biopic called *The Indians' Father Whitehead*, made by Charles Callanan and the Memorial University Extension Service in 1979.

The Indians' Father Whitehead, frame enlargement
1971, dir. Charles Callanan, Memorial University Extension Service
DIGITAL ARCHIVES INITIATIVE, MEMORIAL UNIVERSITY

Between July and September 1929, cameraman Maurice Kellerman joined Captain Bob Bartlett for an expedition along the coasts of Newfoundland and Labrador.[8] Footage from that journey was first released under the title *Bob Bartlett's Labrador* in 1930. British Pathé later incorporated some of this footage into a series of shorts under the title of *In Peary's Footsteps* (1932-3). Footage from the standalone short *With Lipstick and Whatnot in Labrador* (1932) also comes from the film shot in 1930. Here, Kellerman's wife barters goods with Inuit in Saglek Bay in exchange for their agreement to participate in the film.

With Lipstick and Whatnot in Labrador, frame enlargement
1932, dir. Maurice Kellerman
BRITISH PATHÉ

A cameraman with the 1931 MacMillan expedition films across the road from the Moravian Church in Nain and seems to discuss his shot with Nain residents, who have turned out in numbers for the event.

photograph
1931
PEARY-MACMILLAN ARCTIC MUSEUM, BOWDOIN COLLEGE, IMAGE 2004.14.547

Schoolchildren at the MacMillan Moravian Mission School in Nain in 1937. To the right of the frame, behind the railing, missionary Paul Hettasch operates his film camera. The building at left was originally MacMillan's research station from Anaktalak Bay.

photograph
1937, Donald Baxter Macmillan
PEARY-MACMILLAN ARCTIC MUSEUM, BOWDOIN COLLEGE, IMAGE 3000.33.5317

The first woman to shoot film in Labrador was likely Miriam Look MacMillan, the wife of Donald MacMillan. Here, she films in Nain, 1937. In her memoir, *Green Seas and White Ice*, Miriam recalls of 1938: "Our second and last night there brought a real treat for all. A motion picture show. [...] We had several reels which I had taken on the coast the summer before. Since they knew all the actors, it turned into an evening of shrieking, giggling and muttering as one familiar face after another—many right there in the audience—flashed on the screen. A fitting windup to two days of fun and visiting at Nain."[9]

photograph
1937, Donald Baxter Macmillan
PEARY-MACMILLAN ARCTIC MUSEUM, BOWDOIN COLLEGE. IMAGE 3000.33.5403

1940s

The onset of World War II transformed Labrador's relationships with colonial powers. Expeditions by individual filmmakers declined. The majority of 1940s film productions focus on the military development of Goose Bay, which was often presented as a marvel of wartime engineering. Labrador cinema's predominant mode of documentary gave some ground to propaganda, beginning a trend that would continue over the next few decades as industrial and promotional filmmaking took off. The films that chronicle the development of the air base and the community that grew around it are remarkably uniform. They all *tell* us about the significance of construction, but none really *show* us. Beyond the Upper Lake Melville area, several films on Labrador's south coast were taken by the Grenfell Mission and by churchman Lester Burry, who was also Labrador's elected representative to the Newfoundland National Convention of 1948.

An early image of Goose Bay. Fish Hassell was an amateur producer whose work demonstrates a typical representation of the base and community from a military point of view. Other frames include aircraft, livestock, the military chapel, and nearby hills.

Fly North Not East, frame enlargement
dir. Bert R.J. "Fish" Hassell
LABRADOR CAMPUS ARCHIVE

EXIT ONLY
ENTRANCE

The USAAF Base Theatre at Goose Bay, 1943 or 1944. This was one of the first fixed movie theatres in Labrador and the first of three theatres that would operate on the base at Goose Bay.

photograph
THEM DAYS, IMAGE M001.318

A rare still of the dock at Goose Bay from 1943, taken from *Workers at War No. 4*. The National Film Board had been established by the Canadian government in 1939, and produced many short propaganda films in support of the war effort.

Workers at War No. 4, frame enlargement
1943, National Film Board of Canada

One of the more geographically ambitious films produced by the Grenfell Mission, *The Challenge of the Labrador* depicts Mission operations between St. Anthony and Saglek. Here, nurse Dorothy Jupp tends the hospital garden at St. Mary's River, later Mary's Harbour.

The Challenge of the Labrador, frame enlargement
Crawley Films
COURTESY OF CRAWLEY FILMS, LIBRARY AND ARCHIVES CANADA, ISN 228893

1950s

The 1950s saw an explosion of filmmaking in Labrador, both in quantity and diversity of form. Some of the most striking footage from the decade was taken by Richard Leacock, a pioneer of a type of documentary film called direct cinema. Travelling with his wife, Eleanor, who was researching her doctoral thesis, and their two children, Leacock had hoped to create a film in the vein of Robert Flaherty's *Nanook of the North*, working with Innu. Limited by technology and with no fluency in Innu-aimun, Leacock ultimately abandoned the project.

The industrial films chronicling developments of Labrador West and Churchill Falls also experimented with shot composition and editing. Made by companies like the National Film Board of Canada, Crawley Films of Canada, and the US-based Cinécraft, these films presented Labrador as a wild space to be tamed by technology.

Later in the decade, the first live televisions broadcasts were made in Labrador beginning with Canadian Broadcasting Corporation programming and the first local news.

Hamilton Power Survey is the first industrial film to chronicle the development of the Grand Falls. Here, surveyors take measurements along the riverbank in preparation for hydroelectric development.

Hamilton Power Survey, frame enlargement
1958, Crawley Films and British Newfoundland Corporation
COURTESY OF CRAWLEY FILMS, LIBRARY AND ARCHIVES CANADA, ISN 429834

ASTRA
NEXT SHOW
TONIGHT

The Astra, pictured here about 1950, was the second of three theatres that operated on the Goose Bay air base. The building still stands in the now-civilian "North Side" area of Happy Valley-Goose Bay. There was also the Aurora Theatre in Happy Valley, which opened on Kessessaskiou Street in 1956. Other communities had cinemas as well. The movie theatre in Hopedale was originally operated by the American radar base, which opened in 1953, and like the Aurora, it played mainly Hollywood Westerns. After the closure of the base, the projector and seating were moved to the Hopedale community hall.

photograph
THEM DAYS, IMAGE M000.025

During the 1950s and 60s, Moravian missionary Gerhard Vollprecht took home movies mainly within the community of Hopedale. Here, Natan Frieda prepares for Christmas Eve service.

Kirche im Schneesturm, frame enlargement
dir. Gerhard Vollprecht
COURTESY OF THE VOLLPRECHT FAMILY

One of three Labrador films produced by Cinécraft, a production company based in Cleveland, Ohio, *Up the Line in '53* chronicles the construction of the Quebec North Shore and Labrador Railway. The perspective in this shot gives a vivid sense of the landscape in this part of Labrador.

Up the Line in '53, frame enlargement
1954, Cinécraft
COURTESY OF CINÉCRAFT, LABRADOR CAMPUS ARCHIVE

Imagery of the Menihek hydro-electric project does not circulate today as it did in the 1950s and 60s, with more recent and larger projects occupying public consciousness. Nevertheless this shot is dramatic. Cutting across the frame at a 45-degree angle and with an abundance of white water in the foreground, the development thrusts into view.

Ore in '54, frame enlargement
1954, Cinécraft
COURTESY OF CINÉCRAFT, LABRADOR CAMPUS ARCHIVE

Minipi's Discovery contains likely the earliest colour aerial moving imagery of Labrador. Well-known outdoorsman and conservationist Lee Wulff was an avid pilot who understood precisely how aerial photography worked in sporting film.

Minipi's Discovery, frame enlargement
1957, dir. Lee Wulff
COURTESY OF JOAN WULFF

Rutherford Platt took this picture of boys posing with a motion-picture camera in Nain, July 1954. Platt served as expedition botanist for Donald MacMillan. By the time this photograph was taken, Nain residents had a long history of interaction with visiting filmmakers. MacMillan himself had been a familiar face for nearly five decades.

photograph
1954, Rutherford Platt
PEARY-MACMILLAN ARCTIC MUSEUM, BOWDOIN COLLEGE, IMAGE 2014.10.66

1960s

This was a pivotal decade in Labrador cinema. The first films from the 1960s continued the celebration of industrial development in Labrador West and Churchill Fall. Atlantic Films's *Labrador* (1963) takes that celebration to its end, painting all of Labrador as a land of riches, "of contrasts, change, and promise." It is the pinnacle of industrial filmmaking in the region. Additional films chronicling the Lower Churchill Development and the work of the International Grenfell Association followed, but the scope of those films was narrower and their tone less celebratory.

On the north coast, Uncle Jim Andersen began his decades-long work of filming Makkovik. Beginning his work as a documentarian in the 1940s with still photography, by the 1960s Andersen had added moving imagery to his repertoire. Over the next four decades he produced thousands of hours of footage.

Towards the end of the decade, the Memorial University Extension Service began to mobilize film production for local community development. Standalone films came first, followed by the *Labrador Film Project (1969)*, a 14-part series featuring southern Labradorians and their perspectives on local challenges, in the community filmmaking model originally made famous on Fogo Island.

LABRADOR

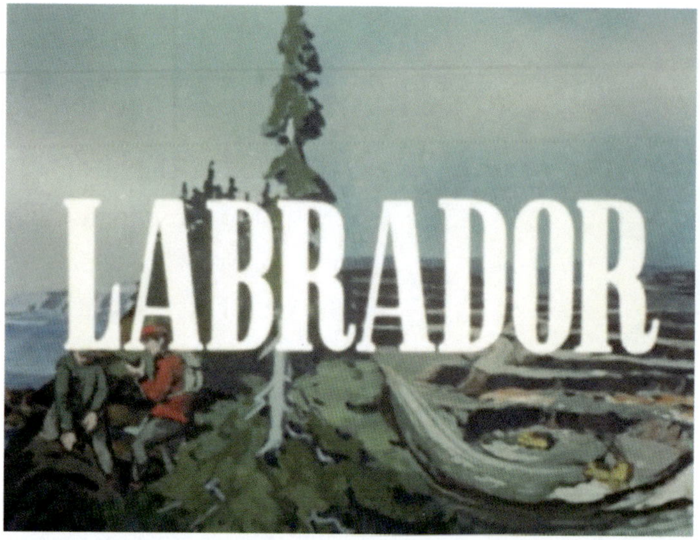
LABRADOR

LABRADOR

LABRADOR

The title sequence for Atlantic Films's 1963 promotional film *Labrador* features an expansive, painted panorama of Labrador landscapes, transitioning from a complex winter scene juxtaposing Inuit with snowhouses and a komatik and Innu with a traditional tent and a canoe, to summer scenes of open pit iron ore mining and hydroelectric production.

Labrador, frame enlargement
1963, Atlantic Films
THE ROOMS PROVINCIAL ARCHIVES OF NEWFOUNDLAND AND LABRADOR

Atlantic Films was part of Premier J.R. Smallwood's vision for "New Industries" in the province following Confederation with Canada in 1949. The Newfoundland-derived, industrial perspective of *Labrador* is on display in this photograph: the St. John's premiere of *Labrador* at the Paramount Theatre on December 16, 1963.

photograph
1963
J.R. SMALLWOOD COLLECTION COLL-285
ARCHIVES AND SPECIAL COLLECTIONS, MEMORIAL UNIVERSITY

Labrador's migratory fishery, an industry vital to Newfoundland since the eighteenth century, has received little attention in film. Here, a crew from the Canadian Broadcasting Corporation films *Voyage to the Sea of Ice* at Ice Tickle, near Indian Harbour in southern Labrador, June 1968. From left to right: Gerry Richardson, Brian Avery, Roger Racine, Peter Mueller.

CBC Times, March 29-April 4, photograph
1968
COURTESY OF CANADIAN BROADCASTING CORPORATION

The *Labrador Film Project* was shot between 1968 and 1970 by a Memorial University Extension Service film crew and featured southern Labrador men speaking on the local economy and community development. Top, from left: (1) Ace Wentzell, Tub Harbour; (2) Jack Keefe, Black Tickle; (3) Ray Rumbolt, Mary's Harbour (left), speaking with interviewer Tony Williamson. Centre: (4) Ray Ward, Snug Harbour; (5) Spotted Island in a scene from "Introduction to Labrador"; (6) Samson Learning, Calloway Cove. Bottom: (7) Solomon Curl, Fox Harbour; (8) "Time for Change", Cape St. Charles; (9) "West Bay People".

Labrador Film Project, frame enlargements
1968-1970, Memorial University Extension Service
LABRADOR CAMPUS ARCHIVE

1970s

The community-oriented filmmaking projects of the 1960s set the stage for much of the filmmaking in Labrador during the 1970s. Memorial University Extension Service had demonstrated that Labradorians could represent themselves on their own terms, even when Labradorians did not necessarily have direct control of the means of production. New political organizations such as the Labrador Inuit Association, the Naskapi-Montagnais Innu Association, the Combined Councils of Labrador, and a Royal Commission on regional governance provided new mechanisms for self-governance. That trend extended into filmmaking. Roger Hart's *Labrador North* (NFB, 1973) and Dave Quinton's *Land & Sea* episode "People of the Torngats" (CBC, 1973) are products of this movement.

In central Labrador, the establishment of Television Community Recreation in North West River and the broadcast of *Directions for Labrador* on the Goose Bay CBC affiliate enabled Labradorians to have public, visual conversations with each other about what was happening in their home. Memorial's Extension Service also continued to produce during this decade, with much of its work documenting Labrador's increasing political and economic organization.

In Labrador West, the Community Recreation Rebroadcasting Service Association began to take shape in 1979. Today, CRRS is primarily a television, internet and telephone service provider, but the company also operates Community Channel 3 for broadcasting public service announcements and covering live events.

A Family of Labrador is a cinematic continuation of Elizabeth Goudie's memoir, *Woman of Labrador*. The film retells the story of Goudie's life and productively contrasts the careers of two of her sons: Horace, who was a well-known trapper, pictured here on his trapline, and Joe, who served in Newfoundland and Labrador's House of Assembly.

A Family of Labrador, frame enlargement
1978, dir. Kent Martin, National Film Board of Canada

CINEMA NORTH

This still from *A Family of Labrador* shows the former Astra theatre, still serving as a cinema 28 years on. Cinema North closed in the late 1970s, around the time that the current Arcturus Theatre opened its doors.

A Family of Labrador, frame enlargement
1978, dir. Kent Martin, National Film Board of Canada

Tom Okkuatsiak at a seasonal fish camp, possibly in Okak Bay. The splitting table is a desk from a Moravian school. *Labrador North* documents the Labrador Inuit response to the 1974 Royal Commission on Labrador.

Labrador North, frame enlargement
1973, dir. Roger Hart, National Film Board of Canada

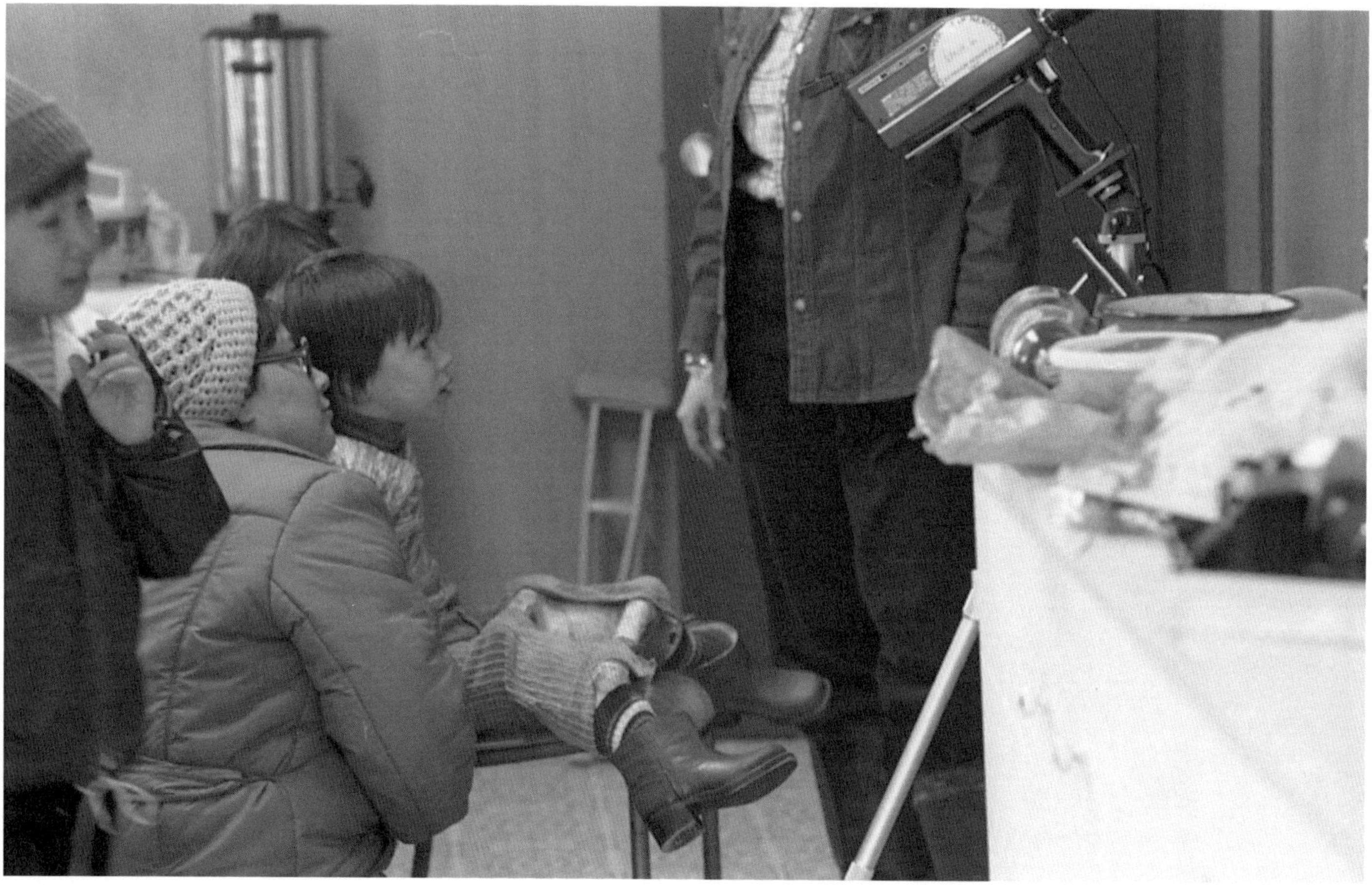

Michael Palliser, Phoebe Fines, and Michael Fines watch video playback in Rigolet, 1978. The footage was shot for *A Doll Making Workshop in Labrador*, produced by Memorial University Extension Service.

photograph
1978, Doris Saunders
THEM DAYS, IMAGE J000.438

A CBC crew prepares for shooting a *Land & Sea* episode at Pack's Harbour, 1978. From left to right: Ralph Pottle, Maurice Coombs (kneeling), Dave Quinton, and Nigel Markham (foreground). Markham went on to make several important films about Labrador.

photograph
1978, Doris Saunders
THEM DAYS, IMAGE N001.017

To celebrate the bicentennial of its Nain mission station, in 1971 the Moravian Church held elaborate celebrations in and around the community. Part of the celebrations was a re-enactment of missionary Jens Haven's arrival at Kauk just to the south of Nain. Left is a photograph from the OKâlaKatiget Society collection. At the bottom left of the image, a cameraman from Memorial University's Extension Service (likely Paul MacLeod) films the re-enactment. Right is a frame from the footage itself. So detailed was the historical pageant that the pre-Moravian contact Inuit were dressed in skin clothing, positioned in skin tents, and even working with skins on-site. Here, one of the performers is working with seal skin, likely preparing kamek (boots).

photograph
1971
OKÂLAKATIGET SOCIETY COLLECTION

unedited footage, frame enlargement
1971, Memorial University Extension Service
DIGITAL ARCHIVES INITIATIVE, MEMORIAL UNIVERSITY

1980s

The 1980s was another bumper decade for media production in Labrador. What changed was the nature of the productions. Nigel Markham and Anne Budgell's *Last Days of Okak* embodies this shift. Released in 1985, it remains one of the most iconic films ever made in Labrador. Constructed from the personal histories of the survivors of Okak, which was decimated by the 1918 influenza pandemic, the film continues to resonate with audiences because of its subjects: Maggie Saunders, Rosie Ford, Emelia Merkeratsuk, and Martha Joshua.

Three years earlier, in 1982, the OKâlaKatiget Society was established in Nain. First a radio service, by 1983 it had also started producing television. *Labradorimiut* began as a five-minute segment on the Inuit Broadcasting Corporation's *Qaggiq* program, before expanding into a thirty-minute standalone show on Television Northern Canada, and finally on the Aboriginal Peoples Television Network. The show ran for 28 years and spanned approximately 500 episodes.

In Upper Lake Melville, the newly established Labrador Institute of Northern Studies (now the Labrador Campus) carried on Memorial University's community development film work. Its first major work was a series called *Speaking Indian with José Mailhot,* co-produced with the Provincial Department of Education and offering filmed instruction on the Innu-aimun language. The Labrador Institute of Northern Studies later embarked on other expansive productions, including *The Labrador Fisheries Co-operative Education Project* in 1984 and *Labradorians at Work* in 1989.

The brass bands of northern Labrador are iconic in Labrador Inuit culture. The Nain Band provides the sombre score for *The Last Days of Okak,* which recounts the tragic loss of life during the 1918 influenza pandemic, and the destruction of the community of Okak.

The Last Days of Okak, frame enlargement
1985, dirs. Anne Budgell and Nigel Markham, National Film Board of Canada

Anne Budgell, author and long-time host with the Canadian Broadcasting Corporation, appears in an episode of the Labrador Institute of Northern Studies's 1989 video project, *Labradorians at Work*. The series profiled professionals from across Labrador to assist young people's decisions about their own education and careers. Here Budgell interviews well-known Inuk educator Beatrice Watts.

Labradorians at Work, frame enlargement
1989, dir. Anne Budgell, Labrador Institute of Northern Studies
LABRADOR CAMPUS ARCHIVE

OKâlaKatiget Society video crew, 1980s. From left to right: Joe Dicker, Gilbert Haye, Alice Pilgrim, Rita Andersen, Johannes Lampe, Sharon Pevie, Gary Baikie. Colloquially known as the "OK Society" across Labrador, OKâlaKatiget is an Inuttitut/Inuttut word often translated as "people who talk or communicate with each other." They remain the only broadcaster working in Inuttitut/Inuttut in Labrador.

photograph
James Andersen
JAMES ROBERT ANDERSEN COLLECTION, ITEM 22.05.677
COURTESY OF THE ANDERSEN FAMILY

The control room inside CBC's television studio in Happy Valley-Goose Bay, 1989. The studio was formerly located at 171 Hamilton River Road, which later housed the Provincial Court of Newfoundland and Labrador.

Labradorians at Work, frame enlargement
1989, Labrador Institute of Northern Studies
LABRADOR CAMPUS ARCHIVE

Diane Beaudry's short documentary *Too Dirty for a Woman* revisits the striking imagery of western Labrador's industrial films to celebrate the contributions of female workers to mining operations in Labrador City.

Too Dirty for a Woman, frame enlargement
1984, dir. Diane Beaudry, National Film Board of Canada

1990s

During the 1990s, the tone of media produced in Labrador changed again. While social issues had been central to media being made in the region since *The Labrador Film Project*, during this decade the stakes of those issues became more apparent. The National Film Board of Canada played a leading role in this shift. Films like Nigel Markham and Hugh Brody's *Hunters and Bombers* (1991), which documented Innu resistance to low-level flying in central Labrador, and John Walker's *Place of the Boss* (1996), made shortly after the People's Inquiry held in Utshimassits, are complex records of Innu communities both addressing loss and asserting sovereignty.

The 1990s also saw the rise of promotional media-making all across Labrador. Unlike industrial films from Labrador West or the films that chronicled the work of the International Grenfell Association, productions like *Cain's Legacy* (1991) and *Labrador: Awaken Your Heart and Soul* (1993) were created to attract tourists to the region, while Labrador Shrimp Fishermen's Union Company's *Realizing the Dream* (1996) documented the long history of the LSFUC.

A public meeting between representatives from the Canadian Government and members of Sheshatshiu Innu First Nation on the issue of low-level flying in central Labrador. Here, Peter Penashue, standing centre, addresses Pierre Cadieux, then Minister of Indian Affairs and Northern Development, seated front and wearing a white jacket, and his entourage.

Hunters and Bombers, frame enlargement
1991, dirs. Hugh Brody and Nigel Markham, National Film Board of Canada

Donna Roberts performs for *The Strever Express,* produced by Television Community Recreation in North West River through the joint provincial/federal Year of the Arts 1997 program. *The Strever Express* ran throughout the year as a series of episodes, each introduced by host Leander Baikie and featuring regular musical performances by the Northernaires and dramatic sketches by the North West River Players, as well as guest appearances by various Labrador musicians.

The Strever Express, frame enlargement
1997, Television Community Recreation
COURTESY OF LEANDER BAIKIE, LABRADOR CAMPUS ARCHIVE

The community development and industrial film genres blend in *Realizing the Dream*, a promotional documentary covering the creation and first 18 years of the Labrador Fishermen's Union Shrimp Company. Here, fish processors work in the plant at L'Anse au Loup.

Realizing the Dream, frame enlargement
1996, Labrador Shrimp Fishermen's Union Company
COURTESY OF LABRADOR SHRIMP FISHERMEN'S COMPANY

Labrador Inuit: The Land, the Sea, and the People is the first of a two-part series commissioned by the Labrador Inuit Association and produced by the OKâlaKatiget Society. Unlike its companion, *Negotiating the Claim*, this film is made up largely of footage produced for the *Labradorimiut* series. It is a rare, wide-reaching introduction to the culture and history of Labrador Inuit told by Labrador Inuit.

Labrador Inuit, Part One: The Land, the Sea, and the People, frame enlargement
1993, dir. Mark Hamilton, Labrador Inuit Association
LABRADOR CAMPUS ARCHIVE

M3A

Gary Baikie, a long-time producer and host of *Labradorimiut,* filming at the old OKâlaKatiget Society studio in Nain.

photograph
OKÂLAKATIGET SOCIETY COLLECTION

2000s

The new millennium saw more films being made by Labradorian filmmakers and commissioned by Labrador-based organizations. Mushuau Innu filmmaker Christine Poker directed three films, *The Child Suffers, but All They See Is a Gas Sniffer* (2000), *My People's Journey / Uetutets Ente Nitsh Innuts* (2004) and *Romancing the Labrador: The Journey of Nutakuan* (2006), while Uncle Jim Andersen's work was the subject of two different retrospectives, *James Andersen: Over Fifty Years of Taking Pictures* (circa 2004), directed by Rhonda Buckley, and *Uncle Jim's Northern Labrador Traditions*, directed by Uncle Jim and Tony Dawson. Before a catastrophic fire diminished its production capacity and destroyed its audio-visual archive in 2005, the OKâlaKatiget Society also produced three major productions, which were all eventually aired as episodes of *Labradorimiut*: Sarah Abel's *A Traditional Seal Hunt in Nunatsiavut* (2001) and Nigel Markham's pair of films about the forced relocation of Hebron, *Forever in Our Hearts: Memories of the Hebron Relocation / Ommatimmiutagennaniattavut: IkKaumset Hebaronimit Notitausimanningit* (2001) and *Without Consent: The Resettlement of Inuit of Northern Labrador / Angimajuka Tinnagu: Notitausimanningi Inuit Labrador Iagganimiut* (2003).

A prolific filmmaker throughout the 2000s and early 2010s, Christine Poker celebrates the resiliency and richness of Mushuau Innu culture. *Uetutets Ente Nitsh Innuts* tells one chapter of the recent story of the Mushuau Innu by documenting the transition from Utshimassits (Davis Inlet) to Natuashish. This image is from a community feast held shortly after the community's move.

Uetutets Ente Nitsh Innuts / My People's Journey, frame enlargement
2004, dir. Christine Poker
COURTESY OF CHRISTINE POKER

The forced resettlements of Nutak in 1956 and Hebron in 1959 are pivotal moments in Labrador Inuit history. To commemorate the fiftieth anniversary of Hebron's resettlement, the OKâlaKatiget Society commissioned Nigel Markham to direct two films on the subject. *Forever in Our Hearts: Memories of the Hebron Relocation / Ommatimmiutagennaniattavut: IkKaumset Hebaronimit Notitausimanningit* (2001) documented a reunion of survivors in the community. *Without Consent: The Resettlement of Inuit of Northern Labrador / Angimajuka Tinnagu: Notitausimanningi Inuit Labrador Tagganimiut* (2003) used dramatic recreations and historical records to examine why the Government of Newfoundland, Grenfell Mission, and Moravian Church moved to close the community. Here, one of the outlying buildings of Hebron is pictured in *Without Consent.*

Without Consent: The Resettlement of Inuit of Northern Labrador / Angimajuka Tinnagu: Notitausimanningi Inuit Labrador Tagganimiut, frame enlargement
2004, dir. Nigel Markham, OKâlaKatiget Society
OKÂLAKATIGET SOCIETY COLLECTION

Long before the Muskrat Falls hydroelectric project brought the lower stretches of river to provincial and national attention, the Grand River was already a site of cross-cultural local advocacy. *Grand River: Labrador's Treasure, Newfoundland's Secret* provides a glimpse of that advocacy and the stakes which would ultimately come into play.

Grand River: Labrador's Treasure, Newfoundland's Secret, frame enlargement
2006, dirs. Brenda Beck and Eric Harris, Grand Riverkeeper
COURTESY OF GRAND RIVERKEEPER

Here James Andersen washes the blood from a newly harvested sealskin in the late 1950s or early 1960s. Uncle Jim documented similar scenes of everyday life across six decades, especially in his home community of Makkovik. *Uncle Jim's Northern Labrador Traditions* was edited by Andersen himself in 2009 and offers a 20-minute montage of highlights celebrating his "memories of life on the land." The clips are set to an original soundtrack by Black Tickle musician Richard Neville.

Uncle Jim's Northern Labrador Traditions, frame enlargement
2009, dirs. James Andersen and Tony Dawson
LABRADOR CAMPUS ARCHIVE

Music recording session with Christine Poker and her son Petapenu in Natuashish for *The Legend of Tshiushuas* (2010, dir. Christine Poker) and *Nutshimit / On the Land* (2010, dir. Sarah Sandring, Nirgun Films).

photograph
November 4, 2009, Sarah Sandring
COURTESY OF SARAH SANDRING

2010s

The social and technological changes of the 2010s radically transformed all forms of media-making in Labrador. The ubiquity of video technology and its ease of integration with social media means that more Labradorians are documenting their experiences. Since launching his YouTube channel in 2013, Andrew Andersen has attracted over 1,000 subscribers. His videos document his experiences on the land in Nunatsiavut. Perhaps the most wide-reaching videos from Labrador to be shared via social media during the 2010s, however, were Justin Brake's Facebook streams from the occupation of the Muskrat Falls worksite in late 2016.

Developments in video technology also made the work of more formal producers easier. During the 2010s, a new generation of filmmakers embarked on community-engaged projects that placed Labradorians directly in the work of production. On the north coast, Sarah Sandring's work with Mushuau Innu resulted in the creation of two films, *Nutshimit / On the Land* (2010) and *Nutak: Memories of a Resettlement* (2014). Jenn Brown from the St. John's International Women's Film Festival led community creations in Hopedale—*Handcrafted Hopedale* (2015)—and Nain—*Katatjanik Utippalianinga / The Return of Throat Singing* (2015). And Ruth Lawrence and Brad Gover from the Nickel Independent Film Festival spear-headed the Rigolet youth-created documentary, *This Isn't Right* (2018).

One of a very few examples of scripted, dramatic performance, *Kuekuatsheu Mak Muak / The Wolverine and the Loon* is a 2013 short film co-directed by Navarana Igloliorte and Christine Poker. It makes extensive use of costumes, make-up, and shooting both outdoors and in tents to create a highly stylized re-enactment of an Innu legend, dramatizing the narrator's Innu-aimun retelling largely through dance and music.

Kuekuatsheu Mak Muak / The Wolverine and the Loon, frame enlargement
2013, dirs. Navarana Igloliorte and Christine Poker
COURTESY OF NAVARANA IGLIOLIORTE

Based on a traditional Inuit sory, *Shaman* is then eighteen-year-old animator Echo Henoche's adaptation of the Polar Bear and the Rock. *Shaman* stands out in Labrador cinema as a rare animated film.

Echo Henoche, photograph
2016, Kat Baulu
© NATIONAL FILM BOARD OF CANADA

Shaman, frame enlargement
2017, dir. Echo Henoche, National Film Board of Canada
© NATIONAL FILM BOARD OF CANADA

Benjamine Rich (left) and Christine Poker filming for *The Legend of Kaianuet*, which tells the story of a young Innu hero who saves his people from the monstrous, human-devouring Maminteu.

photograph
March 16, 2013, Sarah Sandring
COURTESY OF SARAH SANDRING

Nutshimit / On the Land represents a paradigm shift from the many earlier 1990s and 2000s films documenting hardships in Innu life from external, sociological perspectives. Commissioned by the Mushuau Innu Band Council and filmed in Innu-aimun, *Nutshimit* explores and celebrates Innu cultural well-being and traditional intergenerational teachings, mainly by following Innu youth and their grandparents as they spend time away from town, out on the land. In this frame from the film, shot at Border Beacon, Innu Elder Manishan Nui explains to her grandchildren Patnishia Toma and Thunder Nui how to scrape caribou hide to prepare for it tanning.

Nutshimit / On the Land, frame enlargement
2010, dir. Sarah Sandring, Nirgun Films
COURTESY OF SARAH SANDRING

Nutak: Memories of a Resettlement was produced by a similar process as *Nutshimit,* the other main title in the Innu Film Collaboration between Nirgun Films and the Mushuau Innu. Here, interviews and archival materials are presented to Innu Elders in Natuashish to report progress and get community feedback. Elders Manishan and Joakim Nui are on the screen. British sociologist and project partner Colin Samson stands in the background.

photograph
April 11, 2012, Sarah Sandring
COURTESY OF SARAH SANDRING

Epitacia Bruce, "Aunty Pitt," at her home in North West River. Aunty Pitt first came to Labrador in 1965 as a teacher, well before Labrador's now swiftly-growing Filipino community was established. *Becoming Labrador* tells her story along with those of three other families who settled in Happy Valley-Goose Bay in the late 2010s.

Becoming Labrador, frame enlargement
2018, dirs. Rohan Fernando, Tamara Segura, and Justin Simms
National Film Board of Canada

CRB
AUTOMOTIVE
OIL CHANGE
GENERAL REPAIR

The cast of *Last Stop Garage* in a promtional photo. Aired between 2017 and 2019 on Discovery Channel Canada, the show *Last Stop Garage* is a rare example of commercial, entertainment-oriented media-making in Labrador. Leander Baikie, second from left, says that for the cast, *Last Stop Garage* is an "opportunity to share our stories" for "future generations of our people" and "anyone who will listen."

Last Stop Garage, promotional photograph
2017, Discovery Channel

2020s

Despite a pandemic, the early years of the 2020s have seen steady media production in Labrador. The National Film Board of Canada's Labrador Documentary Project, conceived in the late 2010s, has now released two of its four planned films, with the remaining two set to be released within the next year. Ossie Michelin's *Evan's Drum* and Jennie Williams's *Nalujuk Night* both had highly successful premieres, and *Nalujuk Night* won Best Short Documentary at the 2022 Canadian Screen Awards.

Television audiences well beyond the region also continue to show interest in Labrador. Following the precedents of Ray Mears in *Ray Mears's World of Survival* (1998) and Les Stroud in *Survivorman* (2007), ten reality show participants tackle wilderness survival challenges in the 9th season of the History Channel series *Alone* (2022).

EVAN'S DRUM
WRITTEN AND DIRECTED BY OSSIE MICHELIN DIRECTORS OF PHOTOGRAPHY DUNCAN DE YOUNG · SYLVAINE DUFAUX
EDITOR MEIYEN CHAN MUSIC COMPOSER & SOUND DESIGNER JUDITH GRUBER-STITZER
PRODUCERS KAT BAULU · ROHAN FERNANDO · LATONIA HARTERY EXECUTIVE PRODUCER ANNETTE CLARKE
ONF NFB

Ossie Michelin's journalism career spans multiple media, including time spent as a reporter with the Aboriginal Peoples Television Network. Here the theatrical poster for his first film, *Evan's Drum,* frames its subject with central Labrador's land, water, and sky.

Evan's Drum, poster
2021, dir. Ossie Michelin, National Film Board of Canada

As a photographer, Jennie Williams has documented the nalujuk tradition in Nain for many years. That ongoing work served as the basis for her directorial debut *Nalujuk Night*.

Nalujuk Night, photograph
2021, dir. Jennie Williams, National Film Board of Canada

Director David Borish worked with comunities in Labrador to develop *Herd* over a five-year period, documenting the social and cultural effects of the decline of the George River Caribou Herd. This approach expands and updates the model of research-oriented filmmaking developed by Memorial Extension to mobilize community knowledge and perspectives in the 1970s.

Herd, photograph
2022, dir. David Borish
COURTESY OF DAVID BORISH

POSTSCRIPT

We began this book by considering Labrador's cinema as the total of all moving imagery that concerns this place and the people who call it home. We have not defined the cinema in terms of traditional patterns of creation and reception, because in Labrador those patterns do not really apply.

Many art and national cinemas follow the model exemplified by Hollywood. Films are made, people watch them and form opinions, and critics, social media, and advertising help inform those opinions. All of this carries over into how filmmakers approach their next works and how we view those future films. These cinemas are formed from a collection of media texts. However, smaller cinemas often do not work this way.

In Labrador, most films are made either for a special interest, like an industry, or for a commissioning agency based outside the region, like the National Film Board of Canada. Films are typically screened regionally a handful of times and then circulated within their actual target market elsewhere in North America or Western Europe. Alternatively, in the case of locally commissioned productions, active circulation simply ends. A film may live on through small numbers of hard copies in local hands, or occasionally it might be put online. Thus, new filmmakers tend to represent Labrador with little first-hand knowledge of what others have previously produced. And the cycle repeats.

Between 2010 and 2021, we engaged in various ways with digitizing, describing, acquiring, promoting, and interpreting film materials related to the region, mostly through one of the cinema's principal archives at the Labrador Campus of Memorial University in Happy Valley-Goose Bay. Along the way we gained a perspective on filmmaking and film watching in Labrador that we acknowledge to be peculiar to our experience. How one engages with a tradition strongly influences how one sees that tradition, and there are many different relationships with Labrador cinema besides our own.

The idea of recovering traditions from archives is not new. Here in Labrador, this kind of work happens frequently. Publications like Them Days Magazine and the popular Facebook group "Nunatsiavut/Labrador Inuit, Innu and Settler Photos" use historical records to either remind or show us what day-to-day life has been like in Labrador. These outlets create spaces for people to recover traditions together.

Sometimes, specialized archives provide rich documentation that can be used in the revival of specific traditions: for example, Noah Nochasak has referred to the Moravian missionaries' records in his work on Labrador Kajait (kayaks).[10] The archives used by people in Labrador are often, though not always, colonial in nature, with the result that Labradorians frequently read and use the records in ways very different from the records' original purposes. The North Sámi historian Veli-Pekka Lehtola has described this strategy of reading records as one that focuses "on 'small stories' of us and our ancestors rather than 'big histories' of colonial circumstances and contradictions with outsiders' societies."[11]

Labradorians clearly understand their involvement in the creation of these records, and this understanding extends to film. However, while Labradorians read, re-interpret, reclaim, and repurpose many types of records day-to-day, we have yet to see any widespread use of film records.

There are many reasons why this may be the case. Difficulty of access is one: even though many historical films have now been digitized, copyright presents a significant barrier to their distribution. Knowledge of the contents of the archive is another reason: geography and time often limit our memories of what has already been produced, and Labrador films are all too often forgotten not long after they are made. However, there might be another, more fundamental reason.

We suspect that in many cases, the real significance of filmmaking in Labrador might lie in the act of creating the film itself, rather than in watching and sharing the final product. Filmmaking is inherently collaborative, and people involved in Labrador film have often used collaboration on films as a means of learning and coming together. In these cases, conversations amongst contributors become far more important than anything the films might communicate to audiences in other places and times.

However, we also strongly believe in good, public access to the words and works of one's own regional community. Labrador's cinema has a great deal to offer to the audiences and filmmakers of the future. We hope this book will help to promote the cinema and to make it easier for people to discover its already rich and deep-rooted traditions.

NOTES

1 John Berger, *Ways of Seeing* (London: British Broadcasting Corporation and Penguin Books, 1972), 10.

2 Elizabeth Goudie, *Woman of Labrador* (Nimbus: 1996; originally 1973), 196.

3 Jerry White, T*he Radio Eye: Cinema in the North Atlantic, 1958–1988* (Waterloo ON: Wilfrid Laurier University Press, 2009), 6.

4 Paul Hettasch, "Report from Nain, 1928," *Periodical Accounts* (no. 137, 1929), 326.

5 Paul J. Rainey, "Bagging Arctic Monsters with Rope, Gun and Camera," *Cosmopolitan Magazine* (50, December 1910-May 1911), 91-103.

6 "Pittsburgh Explorer is Returning Home," *Pittsburgh Post-Gazette* (October 12, 1913), 12.

7 "Valuable Finds of Timber and Mineral Made on Labrador," *Western Star* (October 31, 1928), 4.

8 Robert Abram Bartlett papers "929 Journal" M8.6 v. 17 Special Collections and Archives, Bowdoin College.

9 Miriam Look MacMillan, *Green Seas and White Ice* (New York: Dodd, Mead & Co., 1948), 109.

10 Noah Nochasak. "Labrador Kajait Within the Moravian Church Records," *Uncommon Bonds: Labrador Inuit and Moravian Missionaries,* August 6, 2021, https://uncommonbonds.org/labrador-kajait-within-the-moravian-church-records/

11 Veli-Pekka Lehtola. "Our Histories in the Photographs of the Others: Sámi Approaches to Visual Materials in Archives," *Journal of Aesthetics & Culture,* 10, no. 4, (2018): 1. doi: 10.1080/20004214.2018.1510647

FILMOGRAPHY

To capture all of Labrador Cinema in a single list would be impossible. The present filmography aims to be exhaustive in its early decades, when commercial media producers were rare in the region. Post-1960, we have included only finished, edited, commercially or institutionally produced films, while omitting known collections of raw footage. Post-1980 our selection is comprehensive but no longer exhaustive, and by necessity omits many productions judged to be of minor significance to the larger story of the regional cinema. These include, for example, narrowly distributed films documenting specific events or research programs.

All films are English-language titles in colour, with sound, unless otherwise noted. Post-1949, the country of production is only noted for films that are not solely Canadian. The term Inuttitut/Inuttut is used for the Labrador dialect of the Inuit language. Inuktut is used for films in other dialects of that language.

1901	*An Esquimaux Game*—American Mutoscope & Biograph Company (USA), b&w, silent
	Esquimaux Dance—American Mutoscope & Biograph Company (USA), b&w, silent
	Esquimaux Game of Snap-the-Whip—dir. Edwin S. Porter, Edison Manufacturing Company (USA), b&w, silent
	Esquimaux Leap-Frog—dir. Edwin S. Porter, Edison Manufacturing Co. (USA), b&w, silent
	Esquimaux Village—dir. Edwin S. Porter, Edison Manufacturing Co. (USA), b&w, silent
	The Esquimaux Village—S. Lubin (USA), b&w, silent
1902	*Panorama of the Esquimaux Village*—S. Lubin (USA), b&w, silent
1908	*Esquimaux of Labrador*—Goodfellow Film Manufacturing Company (USA), b&w, silent
1910	Paul J. Rainey Expedition footage—S. Lubin (USA), b&w, silent
1911	*Eskimos in Labrador*—Edison Manufacturing Company (USA), b&w, silent
	The Way of the Eskimo—Selig Polyscope (USA), b&w, silent
1913	*Through Eskimo Land*—Alfred Ward Birdsall footage (USA), b&w, silent
1919	Centenary celebrations footage—Hudson's Bay Company (Canada), b&w, silent with English intertitles
	Labrador and Newfoundland—Post Film Company (UK), b&w, silent
[1910s]	Donald and Miriam MacMillan footage [several decades, beginning in the 1910s]—USA, b&w/colour, silent
1920	*Heritage of Adventure*—Hudson's Bay Company (Canada), b&w, silent with English intertitles
1926	*Lure of the Labrador*—dir. Varick Frissell (USA), b&w, silent with English intertitles
	P and S on the Labrador—Grenfell Mission
1928	*Unknown Falls: John Kernan's Explorations of Central Labrador*—USA, b&w, silent
	Monsignor Edward O'Brien footage [1928-1940s]—Newfoundland, b&w, silent
1929	*Vom Spreewald zum Urwald* [possibly 1930]—Germany, b&w, silent with German intertitles

[1920s]	Hettasch family footage [1920s-1950s]—Newfoundland/Canada, b&w/colour, silent International Grenfell Association footage [beginning in the 1920s]—Newfoundland/Canada/USA, b&w/colour, silent/English
1930	*Bob Bartlett's Labrador*—UK, b&w, silent with English intertitles *Leipzig Exhibition footage*—Hudson's Bay Company (Canada), b&w, silent with English intertitles *Trading into Hudson's Bay*—Hudson's Bay Company (Canada), b&w, silent with English intertitles
1934	*Governor's Trip to Eastern Canadian Arctic*—Hudson's Bay Company (Canada), b&w, silent with English intertitles Luther G. Holbrook Footage—USA, b&w, silent
1936	*Dr. Wishart's Labrador Journey*—dir. J.S. Wishart (Canada), b&w, silent with English intertitles
1937	*Labrador, Ungava*—dir. Tim Simms *Patrol to the North West Passage*—dir. Richard Finnie (Canada), b&w, silent
1938	*Labrador Adventure*
1939	*The Labrador Mission*
1940	*Northern Neighbours*—Grenfell Mission
1943	*Building and Using an American Airbase*—British Pathé Company (UK), b&w *Workers at War (No. 4)*—National Film Board of Canada, b&w
1946	*Ice Off Starboard*—dir. James V. Stowell (USA), silent with English intertitles
[1940s]	*Fly North Not East*—dir. Bert R.J. "Fish" Hassell (USA), b&w, English commentary added at a later date *Special Memories* [date uncertain, 1930s-1940s]—dir. S.M. Christian (Newfoundland), b&w, silent Rev. Lester Burry film footage—Newfoundland, b&w, silent *The Challenge of the Labrador*—Crawley Films (Canada)

1950	Richard Leacock footage—USA, b&w, silent
1952	*Big Island*—Audio Pictures, Canadian National Railway *Seven Islands*—dir. Gil LaRoche, National Film Board of Canada, b&w, English & French versions
1953	*Eye Witness No. 58*—dir. Grant McLean & Ronald Weyman, National Film Board of Canada, b&w, English & French versions
1954	*Moose for Labrador*—Atlantic Films, b&w *Up the Line in '53*—Cinécraft (USA), Iron From the North *Ore in '54*—Cinécraft (USA)
1955	*Iron From the North*—dir. Walford Hewitson, National Film Board of Canada, b&w *Operation Eclipse II*—dir. David Bairstow, National Film Board of Canada *Road of Iron*—dir. Walford Hewitson, National Film Board of Canada, b&w, English & French versions
1957	Happy Valley-Goose Bay news and community events coverage [incorporated into the CFLA-TV Goose Bay rebroadcast of CBC's St. John's channel, 1957-2012]—Canadian Broadcasting Corporation *Minipi's Discovery*—dir. Lee Wulff *The Precambrian Shield*—dir. David Bennett, National Film Board of Canada, b&w, English & French versions
1958	*Hamilton Power Survey*—Crawley Films of Canada, British Newfoundland Corporation Ltd.
1959	*The Far North: A Donald MacMillan Lecture Film*—dir. Donald MacMillan, Bowdoin College (USA)
[1950s]	James Robert Andersen footage [1950s-2011]—silent & sound *Kirche im Schneesturm* [date uncertain, 1950s-1960s]—dir. Gerhard Vollprecht (Germany/Canada), silent
1960	*Report From Down North: The Grenfell Mission Today*—Sturgis-Grant Productions (USA)

1963	*Iron From Labrador*—dir. Richard Finnie, Wilding *Labrador*—Atlantic Films
1964	*Labrador Diary*—Scott Films Limited *Land and Sea* [1964-, TV series]—Canadian Broadcasting Corporation *Sept-Îles à la recherche de son passé*—Archaeological Society of Sherbrooke, Iron Ore Company of Canada, French
1966	*Cod: Labrador and East Newfoundland*—Memorial University Extension Service, b&w *Labrador Hospital*—dir. Kryn Taconis, National Film Board of Canada
1967	*Power in Perpetuity: The Churchill Falls Project*—dir. Sally Macdonald, Crawley Films *The Labrador Fishery*—Memorial University Extension Service, b&w *To Labrador for Brook Trout*—dir. Lee Wulff, Government of Newfoundland
1968	*Labrador Mission*—CBC Features Film Presentation (Canada), Le train du Labrador *Le train du Labrador*—dir. Arthur Lamothe, Société Nouvelle des Établissements Gaumont, French *Labrador Film Project* [1968-1970, 14-part series]—Memorial University Extension Service, b&w
[1960s]	*Accomplishment in Northern Quebec*—United States Steel International (USA) *Exploration: Iron Ore in Quebec*—United States Steel International (USA) *The Carol Operation*—Iron Ore Company of Canada *The Grenfell Challenge: Adventure and Experience*—Sturgis-Grant Productions (USA) *The Iron Horse Goes North*—Cinécraft (USA)
1970	"Smoker" [episode of *Strachan Series*]—Memorial University Extension Service *Davis Inlet Caribou Hunters*—Memorial University Extension Service, b&w *Power from Labrador*—Crawley Films *The Grenfell Challenge Mission*—Sturgis-Grant Productions (USA)
1971	*Northern Labrador: Nain Fish Plant*—Memorial University Extension Service, b&w *Northern Labrador Fishery Collection*—Memorial University Extension Service, b&w
1972	*Journey to Power*—Crawley Films *Labrador Series #1: Nain*—Memorial University Extension Service, b&w

1973	*Labrador North*—dir. Roger Hart, National Film Board of Canada *Land & Sea* [ongoing Atlantic Canadian TV series, begun in 1973, with 55+ Labrador episodes]—Canadian Broadcasting Corporation
1975	*Energy Forever: Newfoundland and Canada Meeting the Challenge of Labrador Power Development*—Crawley Films "Labrador Agriculture: Odds and Hens" [episode of *Decks Awash*]—Memorial University Extension Service, b&w
1976	*Bilingual Education in Scotland* [comparison with bilingual education in Northern Labrador]—Memorial University Extension Service, b&w *Labrador Resources Advisory Council*—Memorial University Extension Service, b&w North West River community events and news coverage [TV programming, 1976-2001]—Television Community Recreation *The Basque Whalers of Red Bay*—dir. Fred Hollingshurst, Memorial University
1977	*Grenfell of Labrador: The Great Adventure*—dir. Terence Macartney-Filgate, National Film Board of Canada & Canadian Broadcasting Corporation *Labrador Development Corporation*—Memorial University Extension Service, b&w *Labrador Land Use Conference*—Memorial University Extension Service, b&w *Labrador Microwave*—Terra Communications *Labrador: Land Out of Time*—dir. Terence MacArtney-Filgate, Canadian Broadcasting Corporation & National Film Board of Canada *Uranium* [6-part film series]—Memorial University Extension Service
1978	*A Doll Making Workshop in Labrador*—Memorial University Extension Service, b&w *A Family of Labrador*—dir. Kent Martin, National Film Board of Canada *Labrador Nursery Schools*—Memorial University Extension Service
1979	*Directions for Labrador* [TV series]—dir. Roger Nissenbaum, Canadian Broadcasting Corporation *Master of Ungava*—dir. Bernard Beaupré, Ministry of Tourism, Government of Québec, English & French versions *Monsignor O'Brien* [interviews]—Memorial University Extension Service *The Indians' Father Whitehead*—dir. Charles Callanan, Memorial University Extension Service, b&w/colour

[1970s]	*Handicrafts*—Memorial University Extension Service, b&w *Newfoundland and Labrador Heritage Stories: Sir Wilfred Grenfell*—dir. Vladimir Goetzelman, Cinera, colour (animation) *West St. Modeste*—Memorial University Extension Service, b&w
1980	*North to Labrador*—dir. John Foster, Canadian Broadcasting Corporation & Manitou Productions *Speaking Indian with José Mailhot* [12-part series]—Newfoundland and Labrador Department of Education and Labrador Institute of Northern Studies, English & Innu-aimun
1981	*Labrador: A Battle for Survival*—Mid-Canada Communications *M.V. Arctic: Lake Melville Probe*—dir. Derek Norman, MacLaren Plansearch
1982	*Labrador Pastimes: Toys, Games, and Amusements*—Them Days and Memorial University of Newfoundland
1983	*Labradorimiut* [1983-2011; TV series based in Nain with approximately 500 episodes]—OKâlaKatiget Society, Inuttitut/Inuttut & English *I Well Minds the Time* [TV series with 9 episodes]—Canadian Broadcasting Corporation *Mirage*—dir. William B. Ritchie and Nigel Markham, b&w "The Nain Women's Group" [episode of *Take 30 Access*]—dir. Roman Bittman, Canadian Broadcasting Corporation "Red Bay" [episode of *Where Once They Stood*]—dir. Tom Cahill, Canadian Broadcasting Corporation *Unitas Fratrum: The Moravians in Labrador*—dir. Hubert Schuurman, National Film Board of Canada
1984	*Bill Ritchie: Artists of Labrador and Images of Labrador* [2-part series]—Memorial University Educational Television Centre "Frozen Eden" [episode of *Lorne Greene's New Wilderness*]—Greene & Dewar New Wilderness & CTV "Reverend F. W. Peacock" [episode of *Pathways*]—Memorial University Educational Television Centre

1984 cont.	*Seal Fishing*—Labrador Institute of Northern Studies, The Labrador Fisheries Co-operative Education Project *The Labrador Fisheries Co-operative Education Project*—Labrador Institute of Northern Studies, English & Inuttitut/Inuttut versions *Too Dirty for a Woman*—dir. Diane Beaudry, National Film Board of Canada *What Is a Co-op?*—Labrador Institute of Northern Studies, English & Inuttitut/Inuttut versions
1985	"And Preserve the Bone" [episode of *A Thousand Years Will Come Again*]—Memorial University Division of Educational Technology *Akuliaq: Hunting Caribou in Northern Quebec*—dir. Bernard Beaupré, Ministry of Communication, Government of Quebec, English & French versions *The Revenge of Mina Hubbard* [Heritage Theatre series]—dir. Nigel Napier-Anderson, My Country Productions & CHCH-TV *The Basque Whalers of Labrador*—dir. Thomas Cadieux, Adlanut Productions and Société générale du cinéma du Québec, English & French versions *The Last Days of Okak*—dir. Anne Budgell and Nigel Markham, National Film Board of Canada
1986	"LIDC Caribou Hunt" [episode of *Country Canada*]—Canadian Broadcasting Corporation *Invasion of Our Homeland*—dir. Liz MacDougall, Innu Project Working Group & Centre for Art Tapes *Minipi Trout*—dir. Lee Wulff
1989	*Labrador City* [*Community* series]—dir. Ken Pittman, Instructional Materials Section, Newfoundland and Labrador Department of Education *Labradorians at Work* [12-part series]—Labrador Institute of Northern Studies, Mokami Status of Women Council *Mokami Status of Women Council*—dir. Susan McGrath, Labrador Institute of Northern Studies *Newfoundland and Labrador Rural Women's Learning Project: Women and Leadership: Barb Wood*—Newfoundland and Labrador Association for Adult Education & Memorial University Extension Service

[1980s] *Labrador Rediscovered*—dir. Dave Quinton

1990 *A Celebration of Heritage: Songs of Labrador*—Television Community Recreation

1991 *Cain's Legacy*—Canadian Broadcasting Corporation, Piper Stock Productions Limited

Eye of the Storm—dir. Nigel Markham, National Film Board of Canada & Lazybank Productions

Hunters and Bombers—dir. Hugh Brody and Nigel Markham, National Film Board of Canada & Nexus Television (Canada/UK)

Visions of Labrador—dir. Tony Dawson and Herb Brown, Labrador Craft Producers' Association

1992 *Footsteps in the Snow*—dir. Jack Kellum, Butter and Snow Productions, Canadian Broadcasting Corporation

The Power of Nature—The Dream Company

1993 *Labrador: Awaken Your Heart and Soul*—Destination Labrador

Labrador Inuit, Part One: The Land, The Sea, and The People—dir. Mark Hamilton

Labrador Inuit, Part Two: Negotiating the Claim—dir. Mark Hamilton

Puppets Against AIDS—dir. Barbara Doran, Morag Productions & Canadian International Development Agency

Sketches of Our Town: Happy Valley-Goose Bay & North West River—dir. Conrad Beaubien

1994 *Under the Sun: The Two Worlds of the Innu*—dir. Ken Kirby, British Broadcasting Corporation (UK)

1996 *Place of the Boss: Utshimassits*—dir. John Walker, National Film Board of Canada, Triad Film Productions & John Walker Productions

Realizing the Dream—Labrador Shrimp Fishermen's Union Company Limited

The Strever Express [6-episode TV series, 1996-1967]—Television Community Recreation

1997 *Gathering Voices: The Labrador Creative Arts Festival*—dir. Marion Cheeks

In Caribou Country: The Adventures of William Brooks Cabot in Labrador, 1903-1910—dir. Nigel Markham, Lazybank Productions

Ntapueu / I Am Telling the Truth—dir. Marjorie Beaucage, Innu Nation, Innu-aimun with English subtitles

1998 "The Barren Lands" [episode of Ray Mears's *World of Survival*]—British Broadcasting Corporation

Red Bay: Hidden Basque Treasures—Good Earth Productions

1999 *Crossroads of Courage, Battle Harbour* [*HistoryLands: Canada's Heritage Sites* series]—dir. Paul Dalby, Good Earth Productions & History Television

Labrador Creative Arts Festival—ArtSpace TV

Muspun Nipen / Lisa's Hope—dir. Kathleen Winter, New Creation

Saputjinik / Healing Each Other—dir. Fran Williams, School of Continuing Studies, Memorial University

Shamanism and the Shaking Tent—dir. Phillip Nuna and Ted Ostrowski, Innu Nation, Innu-aimun with English subtitles

The Sweat Lodge with Dominic Pokue—Innu Nation, Innu-aimun with English subtitles

[1990s] *Visions of Makkovik*—dir. James Robert Andersen, silent

2000 "Where Time Stands Still" [episode of *Exploring Horizons*]—Arctic Jungle Films

The Child Suffers, but All They See Is a Gas Sniffer—dir. Christine Poker, Innu Nation, Innu-aimun with English subtitles

Torngats: The Hidden Mountains—dir. Albert Karvonen, Karvonen Films

2001 *A Culture Divided: Moravian Missions*—Good Earth Productions

A Traditional Seal Hunt in Nunatsiavut—dir. Sarah Abel, OKâlaKatiget Society, English & Inuttitut/Inuttut

Forever in Our Hearts: Memories of the Hebron Relocation / Ommatimmiutagennaniattavut: IkKaumset Hebaronimit Notitausimanningit—dir. Nigel Markham, OKâlaKatiget Society, English & Inuttitut/Inuttut

Now It's Our Turn: The Spirit of the Labrador Creative Arts Festival—dir. Marion Cheeks

2002 *A Walk in My Dream*—dir. Mike Stevens, ArtsCan Circle and Television Community Recreation

2003 *Archaeology and Traditional Knowledge in Labrador*—dir. Rhonda Buckley & Fred Hollingshurst, Newfoundland Archaeological Heritage Outreach Program and Distance Education and Learning Technologies, Memorial University

Without Consent: The Resettlement of Inuit of Northern Labrador / Angimajuka Tinnagu: Notitausimanningi Inuit Labrador Tagganimiut—dir. Nigel Markham, OKâlaKatiget Society, English & Inuttitut/Inuttut

2004 *The Mushuau Innu: Surviving Canada*—dir. Ed Martin, Best Boy Productions
Uetutets Ente Nitsh Innuts / My People's Journey—dir. Christine Poker, English & Innu-aimun
The Wild Shore [Great Northern Wilderness series]—dir. Tom Radford, National Film Board and GCW Productions
Pien Upunmun / Pien's Dream—Canadian Broadcasting Corporation, Innu-aimun with English subtitles
Wolves of Labrador—dir. Andrew Manske, Karvonen Films

2006 *Grand River: Labrador's Treasure, Newfoundland's Secret*—dir. Brenda Beck and Eric Harris, Grand Riverkeeper Labrador
Romancing the Labrador: The Journey of Nutakuan—dir. Christine Poker, Muinjij Productions, English & Innu-aimun
The Little Festival That Does—dir. Dorrie Brown, Labrador Creative Arts Festival

2007 "Labrador" [episode of *Survivorman*]—dir. Les Stroud
Being Innu—dir. Catherine Mullins, Documentary Educational Resources

2008 *Breastfeeding: Celebrating the Tradition*—dir. Byron Hamel, Nunatsiavut Government
The Last Explorer—dir. Neil Diamond, Rezolution Pictures and Aboriginal People's Television Network

2009 *Free My Spirit*—dir. Navarana Igloliorte, Nunatsiavut Government
Uncle Jim's Northern Labrador Traditions—dir. James Andersen and Tony Dawson, silent

[2000s] *James Andersen: Over Fifty Years of Taking Pictures*—dir. Rhonda Buckley, Torngâsok Cultural Centre, English & Inuttitut/Inuttut versions

2010 *Nutshimit / On the Land*—dir. Sarah Sandring, Nirgun Films (Canada/Germany), English & Innu-aimun
The Legend of Tshiushuas—dir. Christine Poker, Innu-aimun with English subtitles

2011 *Tamanevugut* [TV series, 2011-2018]—OKâlaKatiget Society, English & Inuttitut/Inuttut

2012 *A Legacy for Life*—dir. Kathleen Blanchard, Torngat Wildlife, Plants & Fisheries Secretariat

The Legend of Kaianuet—dir. Christine Poker

The People of NunatuKavut—dir. Mario Blaser, Memorial University

Till We Meet Again: Moravian Music in Labrador—dir. Nigel Markham, Lazybank Productions

2013 *Kitturiaq*—dir. Frank Wolf, Gravywolf Films, English & Inuktut syllabic subtitles

Kuekuatsheu Mak Muak / Wolverine and the Loon—dir. Navarana Igloliorte & Christine Poker, Anorae Productions, Innu-aimun with English subtitles

"Labrador Winter Games" [episode of *Rick Mercer Report*]—Island Edge Inc. and Canadian Broadcasting Corporation

Meshkanu—dir. Andrew Mudge, Black Kettle Films (USA)

Southern Labrador Road Show—dir. Rhonda Buckley and Lisa Rankin, Understanding the Past to Build the Future project, Memorial University

2014 *Nutak: Memories of a Resettlement*—dir. Sarah Sandring, Nirgun Films (Canada/Germany), English & Innu-aimun

2015 *Handcrafted Hopedale*—dir. Mitchell Aggek, Jenn Brown, Troy Maher, Ryan Winters, St. John's International Women's Film Festival

Katatjanik Utippalianinga / The Return of Throat Singing—dir. Heather Angnatok, Matmatil Angnatok, Jenn Brown, Jason Dicker, Joshua Jararuse, Sarah Semigak Lidd, Troy Maher, Caroline Nochasak, Nancy Nochasak, Maxwell Saksagiak, Jennifer Semigak, St. John's International Women's Film Festival

2016 *Tshiuetin*—dir. Caroline Monnet, Canadian Broadcasting Corporation and DESC Images, French with English subtitles

2017 *Labrador Heritage Minutes* [series of 13 shorts]—dir. Morgen Mills and Jared Knight-Fudge, Labrador Institute

Last Stop Garage [TV series with two seasons]—Discovery Channel

Shaman—dir. Echo Henoche, National Film Board of Canada (animation)

2018	*Formation of Inspiration: Nunatsiavut's Inuit Bachelor of Education*—dir. Mark Sandiford, Shelley Tulloch *Labrador Passage*—dir. Peter Marshall, Public Broadcasting Service (USA) "Per Schiff durch Kanadas Eisberg-Allee: Sommer in Labrador" [episode of *mareTV*]—dir. Steven Galling, Norddeutscher Rundfunk (Germany), German *This Isn't Right: A Journey From Protest to Play*—Nickel Independent Film Festival
2019	*Becoming Labrador*—dir. Rohan Fernando, Tamara Segura and Justin Simms, National Film Board of Canada
2021	*Evan's Drum* [Labrador Documentary Project]—dir. Ossie Michelin, National Film Board of Canada *Nalujuk Night* [Labrador Documentary Project]—dir. Jennie Williams, National Film Board of Canada *Skiing the Mealy: A Film By the Loners*—Gripped Outdoors
2022	*Alone* [TV series]—History Channel *Herd*—dir. David Borish *Nakatuenita/Respect*—dir. Kent Martin, Innu Nation and Community Conservation Research Network
[2020s]	*First Inuk Teacher* [Labrador Documentary Project]—dir. Heather Campbell, National Film Board of Canada *Hebron Relocation* [Labrador Documentary Project]—dir. Holly Andersen, National Film Board of Canada

INDEX

This index is intended to help readers quickly find people, places, organizations, and basic concepts that are mentioned in the text. To locate films not included here, see the chronological filmography above.